Caving

M000239070

Caving

Exploring Limestone Caves

Larry Dane Brimner

SCHOLASTIC INC.

New York   Toronto   London   Auckland   Sydney
Mexico City   New Delhi   Hong Kong   Buenos Aires

For my Paseo del Sol and Col. Johnston, friends in Sierra Vista and Fort Huachuca.

For answering my last-minute questions and providing helpful information, I am grateful to David Elkowitz, Park Ranger at Carlsbad Caverns.

To make sure yours is a safe experience, cave with a minimum of two other experienced cavers, make use of all safety equipment, and use care and common sense. The author and publisher are not responsible for injuries or accidents occurring from any caving activities.

Note to readers: Definitions for words in **bold** can be found in the Glossary at the back of this book.

Photo Credits: Cover: © Michael Nichols/National Geographic Image Collection; p. 2: © Russ Finley/Finley-Holiday Films; p. 5t: © Michael Nichols/National Geographic Image Collection, b: © Sisse Brimberg/National Geographic Image Collection; p. 6: © Tom Till/Stone/Getty Images; p. 8: © Michael Nichols/National Geographic Image Collection; p. 9t: © Charles E. Mohr/Photo Researchers, NY; p. 10: © Arizona State Parks; p. 11t: © Clint Farlinger, b: © Michael Nichols/National Geographic Image Collection; p. 12: © E.J. Maruska/Visuals Unlimited; p. 13: © Eric & David Hosking/Photo Researchers, NY; p. 14, 15: © Sisse Brimberg/National Geographic Image Collection; p. 16, 17: © A & L Sinibaldi/Stone/Getty Images; p. 18, 19: © Richard T. Nowitz/Bettmann/Corbis; p. 20t: © C.C. Lockwood/Earth Scenes/Animals Animals; p. 21t: © Jerry Kobalenko/Stone/Getty Images; p. 23t: © Urs Widmer/Kevin Downey Photography; p. 24b: © Kevin Downey Photography; p. 26, 27: © Richard T. Nowitz/Photo Researchers, NY; p. 28: © Michael Nichols/National Geographic Image Collection; p. 30: © Patrice Georges/Gamma; p. 32t: © Joseph H. Bailey & Larry Kinney/National Geographic Image Collection; p. 33: © Michael Nichols/National Geographic Image Collection; p. 34t: © Michael Nichols/National Geographic Image Collection; p. 35: © Stephen L. Alvarez/National Geographic Image Collection; p. 37: © John & Eliza Forder/Stone/Getty Images; p. 38: © Joseph H. Bailey & Larry Kinney/National Geographic Image Collection; p. 41: © Didier Jordan/Photo Researchers, NY; p. 43t: © Kevin Downey Photography; p. 44: © Michael Nichols/National Geographic Image Collection; p. 46: © Peter Beattie; p. 48, 49: © Albert J. Copley/Visuals Unlimited; p. 50t: © Jeff Topping/Getty Images; p. 52: © Michael Nichols/National Geographic Image Collection; p. 53: © Kerrick James/Stone/Getty Images.

The illustration on the cover shows LeChuguilla Cave, the deepest and fourth-longest cave in the United States at Carlsbad Caverns National Park, New Mexico. The photograph opposite the title page shows calcite formations at Carlsbad Caverns National Park.

No part of this publication may be reproduced in whole or in part, or stored in a retrieval system, or transmitted in any form or by any means, electronic, mechanical, photocopying, recording, or otherwise, without written permission of the publisher. For information regarding permission, write to Permissions Department, Grolier Inc., 90 Sherman Turnpike, Danbury, CT 06816.

Copyright © 2003, 2001 by Franklin Watts, a division of Scholastic Inc.
All rights reserved. Published by Scholastic Inc., 557 Broadway, New York, NY 10012.
Printed in the U.S.A.

ISBN 0-531-18672-5

SCHOLASTIC and associated logos and designs are trademarks and/or registered trademarks of Scholastic Inc.

2 3 4 5 6 7 8 9 10   61   12 11 10 09 08 07 06 05 04 03

Contents

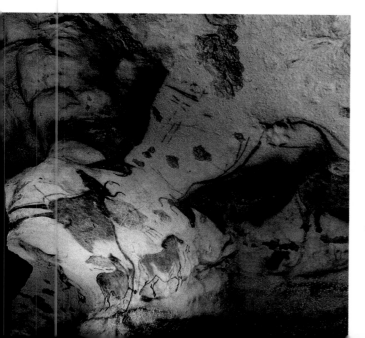

The opening of a cave, such as the Leviathan opening inside the Worthington Mountains in Nevada, can be incredibly large.

Chapter One

The World of Caves

Beneath the surface of the earth lies a world of awesome beauty. It is the underground world of caves. Not all caves are spectacular, but enter the right one, and you'll see an odd and eerie mix of stone formations found nowhere else on earth. Cave forms called soda straws, stone draperies, and cave pearls have taken thousands of years to form. The strange beauty of caves stays hidden to all but the few who dare to explore them.

Decorating a Cave

Natural cave decorations are called **speleothems**, which is a term that comes from the Greek words *spelaion*, meaning cave, and *thema*, meaning deposit. These cave deposits grow over time when water seeps into a cave. The water leaves minerals that build up speleothems, drop by drop.

In limestone caves, common speleothems are **stalactites** and **stalagmites**. Stalactites hang from the ceiling like icicles, and stalagmites grow up from the floor. An easy way to remember which is which is to think of this trick:

A climber studies the stalactites and stalagmites inside Carlsbad Caverns National Park.

Stalactites form downward from drops of water.

Stalactites hang tight to the ceiling, and stalagmites might reach the ceiling! But how do they form?

When it rains, water bubbles down through the soil. On its way, it picks up carbon dioxide from decaying plants and animals. That forms a mild acid called **carbonic acid**. Carbonic acid dissolves limestone and becomes a calcite solution. Calcite is the main ingredient of limestone. The solution flows through small cracks in the top of the cave. It finally reaches the cave's ceiling, where a drop forms. When the water in the drop evaporates, a tiny bit of calcite remains. That's how the stalactite grows.

Speleologists are scientists who study caves. At first, speleologists thought that a stalagmite grew the same way

Bit by Bit

How fast does a speleothem grow? The answer is—very slowly! Speleothems grow about one inch in a hundred years.

9

No Ordinary Straw

Some soda straws grow several feet before breaking off. One of the longest, in Arizona's Kartchner Caverns, is about 21 feet long.

a plant grows. They thought it pushed its way up from under the ground. Now they know that a stalagmite forms the same way a stalactite does. When larger drops of calcite solution form on a cave's ceiling, they become too heavy to hang there, so they splash to the cave floor and evaporate. Again, the calcite is left behind, this time on the floor. If a stalactite and stalagmite both keep growing, someday they will meet and form a column.

Most stalactites are cone-shaped, but soda straws are stalactites, too. They are long and thin with hollow, tube-like centers. Soda straws form when calcite deposits form in a circular shape. A "straw" or tube grows as the solution flows down the center of the calcite circle. As the solution flows, it adds new layers.

Stone draperies are stalactites that hang from a cave's ceiling, but they look like drapes or curtains that might hang in a window. Stone draperies begin with a drop of calcite solution, just as any stalactite would, but sometimes

Clusters of cave pearls (below) and draperies (above) can be found at Carlsbad Caverns National Park.

the cave ceiling is slanted. Then the calcite solution trickles across the ceiling in a tiny stream. These calcite deposits follow this path and form wavy folds and curves. Over time, they become stone draperies.

Cave pearls form the same way that oyster pearls do—around a grain of sand or some other sediment. Sitting in pools, cave pearls begin to take shape when calcite clings to a grain. Water dripping from the ceiling keeps the calcite pearls moving. This motion grinds and smoothes the surface. That is what makes these deposits look round and polished like pearls.

Cave Visitors and Dwellers

Speleothems are not the only wonders that exist inside caves. Caves provide shelter for a rare mix of animal life.

The Dragon Connection

Does this translucent white salamander look like a baby dragon? That's what many people in seventeenth-century Europe thought!

A bat leaves a cave to look for food.

These aurochs, ancestors of domestic oxen, were painted on the walls of Lascaux Cave in France.

The most famous cave animal is the bat. Living in darkness, the bat uses **echolocation**, which is a kind of built-in sonar system. Bats send out high-pitched chirping sounds. These sounds bounce off objects, forming echoes. The echoes guide bats safely through the dark caves. Many kinds of bats live in caves. They give birth and raise their

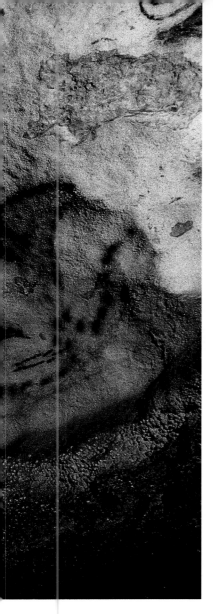

young in caves. At night they leave their caves to look for food. Echolocation helps them hunt in the dark. During winter, the bats stay in their caves to hibernate.

Animals that live their whole lives in caves are called **troglodytes**, or cave dwellers. Troglodytes include some types of flatworms, crayfish, salamanders, shrimp, and beetles. These animals are blind and colorless. To survive in a world of total darkness, they may have long antennae or extra-sensitive nerves to help them find their way around.

Primitive art is another treasure that cavers might find, especially in the caves of France and Spain. More than three hundred pictures were found in the Chauvet Cave in France, including pictures of woolly rhinos, horses, elk, bears, and lions. Some experts believe these pictures were painted with plants and animal blood. They also think that the artists spat their paint onto the cave's rocky surfaces. The pictures may be more than thirty thousand years old. No one knows why people painted in the caves, but we do know that the artists must have had a difficult job. They would have had to crawl on their bellies with only fire torches for light.

Antelope Canyon in Arizona was formed by water.

Chapter Two

How Caves Are Formed

Caves are found almost everywhere in the world. How they were formed depends on the kind of rock from which they were made.

Wind, Water, and Nature

In the American Southwest, stone caves are common. Most were carved by a mix of wind, rain, and moving water. At the bases of cliffs, the sandstone is weaker, so many caves formed there. Sandstone caves are drier than many other kinds of caves, which made them good places of shelter in earlier times. The **Anasazis** were an early people who lived in the Four Corners part of the United States. That's where New Mexico, Arizona, Utah, and Colorado come together. They built elaborate cliff dwellings in the mouths of sandstone caves.

Most caves form slowly over time, but lava caves form quickly. When a volcano erupts, it spews hot lava from its mouth. The lava spills down the volcano's slopes and forms rivers of melted, fiery rock. When the outer layer of lava cools, it forms a crust. Beneath the crust, molten lava continues to flow from the volcano. When the eruption is over, the lava drains from beneath the crust, and a tube-like cave remains.

Lava tubes may be many miles in length, and they may branch out in several directions. They may contain rooms with ceilings that are 80 feet high, or they may be so small that cavers must crawl on their bellies through them. An entrance to a lava tube may form when part of the crust collapses.

No calcite speleothems decorate lava caves, but these caves have amazing formations of their own. Lava-cicles

resemble stalactites and hang from the ceiling. Lava falls, a lava flow frozen in motion for all time, may ripple 30 feet down a wall. Since lava rock is very sharp and jagged, special care must be taken when exploring tubes.

Littoral caves, or sea caves, form in the same way as sandstone caves. They are carved out by wind and moving water. Almost every coastline is dotted with sea caves.

Rosh Hanikrah Sea Caves in Israel are littoral caves that the Mediterranean Sea formed.

19

This diver explores the underwater caves at Naharan Cenote Quintana Roo in Mexico.

Waves blast against coastal cliffs. They wear away the weaker rock, and in time, caves form. Littoral caves may be the most dangerous caves to explore, since tides can catch explorers by surprise. Water can quickly fill the entrance, and the exit, of a cave.

Underwater caves began as dry caves, forming above sea level. They formed before the great ice sheets that blanketed North America and Europe began to melt, forty thousand years ago. The melting ice caused ocean levels to rise, filling some dry caves with seawater. Like littoral caves,

underwater caves are risky to explore. Cave divers need special equipment. If they are not careful, they may kick up silt, clouding the way out. Explorers who get lost can run out of air.

Most glacier caves form high in the mountains. Melted ice water seeps into cracks in the ice, where it melts away layers of ice underneath. The fracture grows large in size. Inside a glacier cave the walls are milky white and ice blue, and they become decorated with stalactites and stalagmites as water drips and refreezes. Cavers explore glacier caves during the colder months when the caves are less slushy. They

Some ice caves are massive, as this one on Ellesmere Island, Canada.

21

The Evidence

How do speleologists know that many underwater caves were originally above sea level? First, many underwater caves have formations that could only have been formed in a dry cave. Second, some underwater caves contain evidence of being used by early people for shelter and burial sites. Early people did not have diving equipment, so they must have used these caves before the sea level rose and flooded them.

wear warm clothing to protect themselves from the cold. They also need to have special mountaineering equipment and experience.

Limestone Caves—Favorites Among Cavers

The giants among caves, and the most commonly explored, are limestone caves. They grow to huge sizes. Some are linked by tunnels and pathways to form cave systems that are hundreds of miles long.

Limestone is a sedimentary rock found all over the world. It's called *sedimentary* because it's made up of sediment—mostly decaying plants and animals that settled to the bottom of the ocean. Movement of the earth's crust, over millions of years, pushed some of the limestone up into mountain ranges, and the pressure of this movement left faults and cracks in the limestone.

Areas where limestone caves have formed are called

karst lands. They are named after an area in Croatia and Slovenia where many limestone caves are found. To form karst lands, two ingredients are needed: limestone and water.

When rain water flows into cracks in the limestone, some of the limestone dissolves into the water. The solution it forms is called carbonic acid. The acid is **corrosive**, which means it eats away at limestone even more easily. The solution flows to the lowest point it can find. Since

These shells in the limestone are fossils, or the remains of animals from long ago. They make up the sediment in limestone.

The Grandest of Cave Systems

With more than 350 miles of mapped paths, Kentucky's Mammoth Cave is thought to be the longest cave system in the world. It may be at least three times longer than any other known cave system. Parts of the cave system are still unexplored. Geologists estimate that as many as 600 miles of unknown passageways may remain.

Ancient artifacts and human mummies have been found in Mammoth Cave. They show that people knew about and explored the cave as much as 4,000 years ago. Over time, however, they forgot about it. Then in 1798, it was rediscovered by Stephen Bishop (1780–1850), an African-American slave (right). Bishop made detailed maps of the cave's passageways and guided tours through it after the owner opened it to the public.

Bishop's keen familiarity with the cave served another important historic purpose. Bishop was an agent for the Underground Railroad, a secret antislavery movement during the 1800s. Bishop often used the cave's many passageways to hide runaway slaves who were on their way to freedom in the North.

limestone caves are formed, in part, by this solution of carbonic acid, they are sometimes called solution caves.

Carbonic acid doesn't work alone to form limestone caves; underground streams also help broaden and deepen them. After many years, these streams either dry up or find another path.

Because limestone caves are created in two ways, they are the grandest caves of all. Their size offers cave explorers the chance to discover and chart new passageways, even inside caves that have already been heavily explored. This is what makes limestone caves a favorite.

A visitor explores Luray Caverns, a show cave, in Virginia.

Chapter Three

Basic Gear

Beginners who want to try caving, or **spelunking**, should begin with a **show cave.** Show caves are safe caves that are open to the public. They give everyone an opportunity to enjoy the wonders of caves. No special gear is needed— comfortable shoes will do!

A show cave unfolds the geologic marvels that lie beneath the earth's surface. It may also spark an interest in exploring **wild caves** and the secrets waiting there.

"Roughing It" the Show Cave Way

Show caves have stairways, paths, and dramatic lighting. That way visitors don't have to crawl through the mud or carry their own sources of light. Some show caves even have elevators to whisk guests to various levels and underground cafeterias that serve lunch!

A Cave's Three Parts

Caves have three parts: the entrance, the twilight zone, and the dark zone. A cave's entrance may be large or small; it may be visible or hidden by dense plant growth. It may be an opening in the side of a hill or mountain, or it could be a pit on the surface of flat land. Cave entrances, and twilight zones, have long been used as shelter by both people and animals.

The twilight zone is also called the **variable temperature zone**. It stays cool year-round just like a cellar or basement. Snakes, skunks, and other animals take shelter there from the daytime heat in summer. Some light filters in from the entrance, so some green plants may grow there. Deeper into the twilight zone, the light becomes dimmer. Green plants give way to fungi and molds.

The dark zone is—that's right—totally DARK! There is no light at all, which means there are no green plants. The animals that live here have adapted to their world of darkness. Some of the animals that live in the dark zone include beetles, fish, salamanders, and spiders. Deep within the earth, the dark zone's temperature stays constant year-round. It can be cool or cold depending upon the cave's altitude and distance from the equator. Further away from the equator and sea level, caves become colder. The dark zone is what daring cavers seek when they begin their adventures. It is the cave's treasure chest of wonders.

Getting Ready

To explore a cave entrance, or even the twilight zone, a caver may not need a lot of special equipment. Often, a light source and good shoes will be enough. Exploring the dark zone is a different story.

A caver, wearing a helmet with many flashlights, prepares himself for a very dark cave.

- **Light** To explore the dark zone, cavers obviously need light. Unlike bats, people don't have echolocation! Cavers should carry at least three different light sources. The most important light source is attached to the helmet. The rest are referred to as backup lights. They can be hand-held flashlights, battery-operated lamps, or carbide lamps. Carbide is a chemical that gives off a gas when mixed with water. It looks like small pieces of dark, gray gravel.

Each type of light source has advantages and disadvantages. Batteries are bulky, so in a tight situation, such as a narrow passageway, a battery-operated lamp may get in the way. Cavers may need to leave these lamps behind as they go further into the cave. Batteries are also heavy, which can become a problem

Scorched Seat Syndrome

Be careful. Carbide lamps can cause "scorched seat syndrome." That happens when one caver follows too closely behind another, and the carbide lamp burns the caver in front!

during long cave outings.

Carbide flames will burn for only about four hours, so extra carbide must be carried to refuel the lamp. The extra carbide must be carried in a water-tight container, because any contact with water will cause the carbide to produce acetylene gas. The gas may catch on fire from the slightest spark. Also, carbide flame lamps frequently break down, so most cavers who use carbide lamps carry a small repair kit and replacement parts. Another disadvantage of carbide is that it leaves behind a toxic residue. This poison must be carried back out of the cave.

So which light is better? Some say that battery-operated lamps are simpler to use. Others say that carbide lamps give off a brighter light. Some use several electric lights to produce more light than a carbide lamp. In the end, each caver must make his or her own choice. More experienced cavers will gladly share their opinions with beginners.

• **Helmet** A helmet with a light on it is NOT optional. One should be worn at all times when caving. The helmet will protect a caver's head from falling matter and sharp rocks. The helmet must include a chin strap, otherwise, it could fall off during a climb and possibly injure someone

A caver always wears a helmet and gloves while exploring a cave.

below. A plastic hard hat is not good enough. Specialty stores sell helmets designed just for cavers.

• **Gloves and Pads** Gloves protect hands from sharp, jagged rocks. They also prevent rope burn when climbing. Most cavers use soft, unlined leather gloves. They also use pads—either the kind that skateboarders or gardeners wear. Pads are bulky, but they save wear and tear on caving clothes. Some cavers sew thick leather patches over the knees of their outer clothing in place of the bulky pads.

• **Rope** Caves can be horizontal, vertical, or a combination of both. When moving between levels, cavers use ropes. Vertical caving requires special equipment and techniques. Only very experienced cavers should try it.

Most cavers buy rope that has nylon kernmantle construction. That means the rope consists of a core (kern) and a braided cover (mantle). Nylon gives a rope great strength and durability. Unlike rock-climbing ropes, which stretch to absorb the impact of a fall, caving ropes stretch very little.

Ropes should be kept in top shape. They should be kept dry and out of sunlight. Cavers should check ropes with their eyes and fingers before each trip. A rope with any frays or lumps needs to be replaced. Ropes should be kept far away from chemicals. Battery acid can destroy the rope's core, even though the damage can't be seen. A rope is a caver's lifeline.

• **Harness** Today, most cavers rely on harnesses to lower themselves into caves. A harness fits snugly around the waist and thighs. They are made from wide nylon webbing.

This caver coils a 600-foot-long caving rope that will support 8,000 pounds.

A photographer, held up by a harness, takes pictures inside a cave.

Since harnesses vary, it's important to follow the maker's instructions for attaching the rope.

- **Carabiners** A carabiner, sometimes called a biner (pronounced "beaner"), is an aluminum or steel link with a locking gate. A biner is used to make connections, usually between the caver's rope and something else, such as the harness.

- **Descenders** When cavers go down into a cave, they don't want to fall too fast—they want to stay in control. The key to a controlled drop is the descender. A descender has one job—to control the flow of the rope. It slows the rope with friction, which acts like a brake. It drags on the

Wearing a helmet, boots, and knee pads, a caver sorts his gear connected to many carabiners during a climb in Snail Shell Cave in Borneo, East Malaysia.

Going Down

Jim White (1882–1946) decided to explore deep into Carlsbad Caverns (New Mexico). Back in the early 1900s, harnesses had not been invented, so White used a bucket for collecting bat guano, or fertilizer, from the cave.

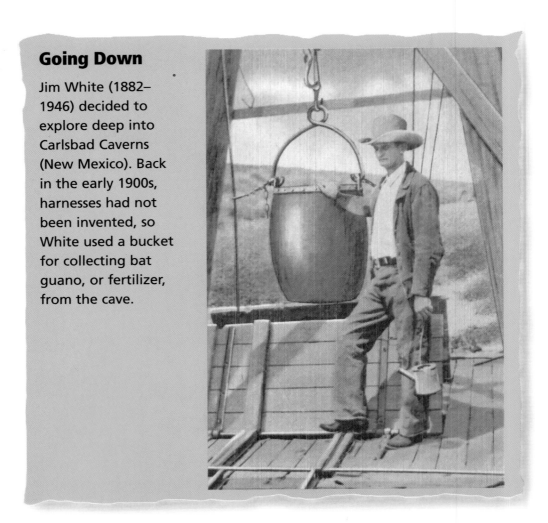

rope the same way that dragging feet can slow down a bike. Descenders let the caver drop at a safe speed. Descending into caves is called **abseiling**.

Cavers can choose from several different kinds of descenders, including figure eights, racks, and bobbins. Cavers choose the one they need based on their experience and, probably, the advice of their caving buddies.

- **Ascenders** Once cavers abseil down into a cave, at some point they need to get back up! One way up is to climb the rope hand over hand, which takes a lot of strength, so most cavers use ascenders.

Ascenders, or jammers, slide up the rope in one direction. They have ratchet devices that usually work by spring action to lock them in place, which prevents them from slipping back down. Most cavers need two or three ascenders to hold their weight, depending on their rigging.

Modern technology makes caving easier and safer than it used to be, but this new equipment comes with a price. Caving is not a cheap sport.

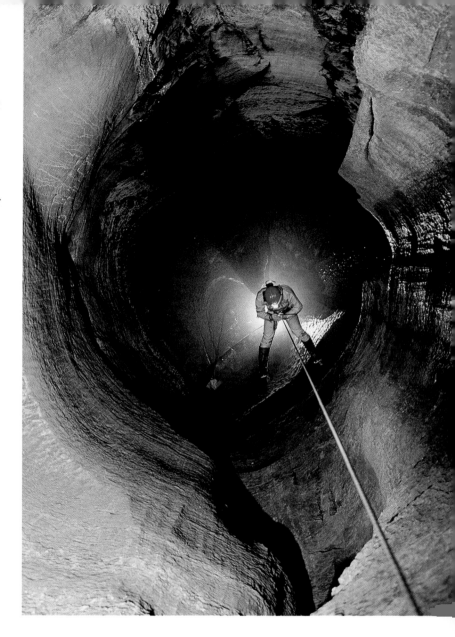

A caver abseils down Notts Pot Cave in England.

These young cavers sit in a low cave, holding carbide lamps, which they have detached from their helmets.

Chapter Four

Safe Caving

Caving can be dangerous, but smart cavers cut down on the risks with training. One way to learn is by joining a caving group at a local college or university. Some Sierra Club chapters, YMCAs, and scouting troops sponsor group outings. The National Speleological Society (NSS) can provide information about local groups, too. Beginning with a group is a good way to pick up advice and skills. In addition to knowledge, some cavers will even share their equipment, which is great for beginners because they may not want to spend a lot of money until they're sure caving is for them.

Before visiting an area known for its caves, it's a good idea to check with the local visitors' bureau. The bureau can tell you if classes for beginners are offered. Many areas of karst lands offer half-day and full-day outings led by experienced guides. Safe equipment is usually included in the fee.

In the end, experience is the key to safe caving.

Dress the Part

Experienced cavers know how to make sure an outing is safe and comfortable. The first rule is to dress the part. In addition to caving gear, cavers need warm, sturdy clothing. Shorts and T-shirts will not do, except for a brief time in the warmest and driest of caves.

Hypothermia, a condition caused when the body's temperature drops too low, is one of the greatest threats to cavers. In severe cases, the victim may freeze to death. Wearing layered clothing can help prevent this from happening. Most cavers today wear underclothing made of polypropylene, the same material that skiers wear under their ski outfits to keep them warm and dry. Thermal underwear will also do the job. Cavers who are familiar with the area will be able to suggest the best clothes to wear.

On top of undergarments, cavers wear zippered coveralls made of denim or strong nylon, the same material used for backpacks. Zippers are better than buttons. They help keep out the mud, and they won't snag on rocks. It's

The Cavers' Motto

The cavers' motto is, "Take nothing but pictures. Leave nothing but footprints. Kill nothing but time."

also a good idea to carry a change of dry clothing in a pack—just in case.

Many people wear sneakers on their first few outings. Sneakers are comfortable in the beginning, but they don't offer the support and protection that feet need during longer caving trips. Ankle-high boots will protect feet from cold and scrapes. Today, most cavers wear boots with light-colored soles. Boots with black or dark soles can leave behind scuff marks. Remember the motto: Leave nothing but footprints.

Boots should fit snugly because loose-fitting boots or boots that are too tight may cause blisters. Snug-fitting boots should be worn with two pairs of socks. A pair of athletic socks is worn against the skin with wool socks on top. Two pairs keep feet dry, and they also help minimize blisters.

Cavers must wear protective undergarments and overgarments when exploring a cave.

Use Your Head

The right clothing can make caving more comfortable, but accidents will happen. That's why cavers carry first-aid kits and learn how to use them. The local YMCA or Red Cross are good places to ask about classes in first aid. At least one person in the caving group should understand first aid, and if more know first aid, that's even better. Also, each caver should have a compass and know how to use it. It's a good idea to carry four plumber's candles and waterproof matches, too. In an emergency, candles can provide light and warmth. When underground, cavers should use common sense and think before acting. Caving is meant to be a fun, enjoyable adventure. Paying attention and being careful helps keep it that way.

Caving Guidelines

- Don't cave alone. Go in a party of three or more, with at least two members being experienced adult cavers.
- Be aware of the weather. Some caves can flood. Being in a cave is a bad idea if a storm is coming.
- Always let another person know where you are going. Tell them when you expect to come back. Stick to that plan.
- Never "free" climb. Climb only with the aid of a rope.
- Never use alcohol or drugs before entering a cave.
- Don't play practical jokes, as they may put you or another person at risk.

The Caving Code

There was a time when people didn't think much about the environment. Some people threw garbage inside caves. Others would break off a soda straw for a souvenir. Some carved their initials into a stalagmite to leave their mark, or tossed pennies into a pool for good luck. Today, we know those actions are selfish and harmful. All cave explorers deserve to see caves in their natural beauty. It should not be spoiled by slobs, graffiti artists, or souvenir hunters.

Today, cavers know that caves must be kept in their

Graffiti can destroy the beauty of a cave.

A caver steps lightly inside a cave. She takes great care not to damage or disturb the cave environment.

natural state. Aside from offering the visitor amazing sights, they have an important purpose. They are part of the **aquifer system**. An aquifer is a natural, underground reservoir. Surface water travels through caves on its way to the aquifer, which supplies drinking water to homes and irrigation water to farms. When we protect our caves, we help protect our water supply.

Caving opens up a new world filled with age-old beauty. A responsible caver respects that world and wants to keep it beautiful for cavers of the future to enjoy.

Lake Cave in Western Australia

Chapter Five

Finding Caves

Caves are found in every part of the world. More than two hundred caves in the United States are open to the public. Show caves, such as Wind Cave (South Dakota), Mammoth Cave (Kentucky), and Luray Caverns (Virginia), give anyone the chance to explore caves. It's not the same as seeing a wild cave, but it offers a glimpse into the wonders of caving. The Jenolan region of Australia, near Sydney, boasts about three hundred caves. Several of these are show caves that are open to the public. Most show caves offer guided tours that offer facts about how caves are made and explored. If an area has caves, its local chambers of commerce and tourism boards will have information about caving attractions.

The Wild Side

After a while, many people find that show caves are not enough. More adventurous types will want to belly-crawl into deeper, unknown regions. They'll want to do some serious spelunking and explore wild caves.

The National Speleological Society has information about local caving places that most people don't even know about. The NSS is an organization that is connected with the American Association for the Advancement of Science. It was formed to find, study, and conserve caves. Members often form tight groups. They meet at local chapters to share information and experiences.

These cavers explore a cave by canoe to study its mysteries.

A Secret Revealed

In 1974, Randy Tufts and Gary Tenen discovered a **live cave**. In live caves, water is still running through and forming speleothems. The live cave, in the Whetstone Mountains of Arizona, was on land owned by the Kartchner family. At first, Tufts and Tenen kept quiet about their discovery, but in 1978 they told the Kartchners about their find. Thus began one of the longest-kept secrets in caving. For fourteen years, only a small circle of friends knew about the Kartchner Caverns, as the cave is now called.

Finally, Tufts and Tenen, along with the Kartchners, realized the caverns were too special to keep secret. The land was turned over to the state. In 1988, the Arizona legislature founded the Kartchner Caverns State Park. It opened to the public in 1999.

Today, Kartchner Caverns is a show cave, but most of it is being kept in its natural, wild condition. It is hoped that as a state park, it will be protected for the future. This way, cavers can enjoy it for many years to come.

Caving is mostly an adult sport, but experienced cavers are happy to introduce young people to caving. They enjoy talking about their favorite local caves, and are sure to welcome anyone who wants to learn from their caving adventures.

Most caves are privately owned. Because of this, cavers need permission from the owners to explore them. Many owners are willing to give permission, but some have been put off by rude cavers. Some cavers don't show respect for private property, and some owners have gotten tired of picking up litter left behind by thoughtless visitors.

When asking for permission to explore a cave on private property, the group should also ask where to leave its vehicles. Cavers shouldn't park in the owner's way. When on private property, the group should stay on paths, if they exist. In short, they should act like good guests. And if the owner says no caving, the group needs to respect that decision, too.

The Caver's Notebook

Experienced cavers soon see that there's more to an outing than just exploring a cave. Most cavers feel it is their duty to chart a cave's passageways or to sketch a cave's formations. These records offer more than memories. Like a map, a caver's notebook entries may chart the course for future cavers.

Every year, new caves are discovered. Some caves thought to have been fully explored reveal new passageways. The lucky caver who first charts a discovery gets to name it!

Cavers like to keep a journal or diary, writing notes or charting maps of their cave explorations.

Caves offer more than a fun climbing experience, or a chance to explore an eerie place. They are a strange and quiet world beneath the earth's surface. Maybe someday you will get the chance to discover one for yourself.

A kayaker explores Emerald Cave in Black Canyon on the Colorado River in Arizona.

Glossary

abseiling—descending, or going down, into a cave

Anasazis—an ancient people who once inhabited cliff dwellings in the Four Corners area of New Mexico, Colorado, Arizona, and Utah

aquifer system—a natural, underground reservoir that supplies drinking and irrigation water

carbonic acid—a mild acid formed when carbon dioxide, a product from decaying plants and animals, dissolves in water

corrosive—something, such as acid, which is capable of wearing away something else

echolocation—a natural, built-in sonar system that enables bats to navigate by sending out sounds and listening for their echoes

hypothermia—a serious condition where the body loses more heat than it generates

littoral caves—sea caves found in coastal cliffs

live cave—a cave that is still forming and evolving through the seepage of water

show cave—a cave commercially developed for tourists

speleologists—scientists who study caves

speleothems—cave decorations made by mineral deposits

spelunking—the exploration of caves and caverns

stalactites—mineral deposits that form on the ceilings of caves

stalagmites—mineral deposits that form on the floors of caves

troglodytes—animals that spend their entire lives in caves

variable temperature zone—the twilight zone of a cave, where the temperature fluctuates

wild cave—a cave in its natural state

To Find Out More

Books

Gibbons, Gail. *Caves and Caverns*. San Diego, CA: Harcourt Brace & Co., 1993.

Gurnee, Russell H. *Gurnee Guide to American Caves*. Teaneck, NJ: Zephyrus Press, 1980.

Jacobson, Don, and Lee Stral. *Caves and Caving*. Boyne City, MI: Harbor House Publishers, 1986.

Judson, David, ed. *Caving Practice & Equipment*. Leicester, England: British Cave Research Association/Cordee, 1995.

Pinney, Roy. *The Complete Book of Cave Exploration*. New York: Coward-McCann, Inc., 1962.

Schultz, Ron. *Looking Inside Caves and Caverns*. Santa Fe, NM: John Muir Publications, 1993.

Silver, Donald M. *One Small Square: Cave*. New York: W.H. Freeman & Company, 1993.

Silverman, Sharon Hernes. *Going Underground: Your Guide to Caves in the Mid-Atlantic*. Philadelphia: Camino Books, Inc., 1991.

Online Sources

Carlsbad Caverns National Park
http://www.carlsbad.caverns.national-park.com/
This site has information about the history of Carlsbad Caverns, as well as information about activities and tours.

The Cave Page
http://www.cavepage.magna.com.au/cave/
This site offers articles about caving in Australia and Europe, plus links to other caving Web sites.

Kartchner Caverns State Park
http://www.pr.state.az.us/parkhtml/kartchner.html
This site details the discovery and long-kept secret of Kartchner Caverns, as well as information about tours.

Mammoth Cave National Park
http://www.nps.gov/maca/home.htm
This site contains detailed information about Mammoth Cave, from its discovery to current maps of its passageways.

Organizations

American Cave Conservation Association
P.O. Box 409
119 East Main Street
Horse Cave, KY 42749
http://www.cavern.org
This group is dedicated to the conservation of caves and ground water supplies through education.

The National Speleological Society
2813 Cave Avenue
Huntsville, AL 35810
http://www.caves.org
The purpose of this club is to find, study, and preserve caves.

Sierra Club
85 Second Street, 2nd Floor
San Francisco, CA 94105
http://www.sierraclub.org
This organization promotes the enjoyment and conservation of the natural environment.

A Note on Sources

When I research any topic, I think it is important to gather as many sources as possible. If I am personally unfamiliar with the topic, my first stop is the children's room of a good local library. Children's books, I've discovered, have a remarkable way of distilling information and making it clear. Thus armed with a basic knowledge of the topic, I then read as many technical books by experts and authorities as possible. For this particular book, my search led me to David Judson's *Caving Practice & Equipment*, Roy Pinney's *The Complete Book of Cave Exploration*, and Sharon Hernes Silverman's *Going Underground: Your Guide to Caves in the Mid-Atlantic*. I also keep alert to articles in newspapers and magazines. Online articles, such as "Cave Creatures Endangered" by Lee Dye for ABCNews.com, which suggested that compromised cave systems might spell trouble for our aquifers, help fill in any gaps.

I also gain knowledge about a topic by speaking with experts and practitioners in the field. Typically, people are eager to share knowledge of their specialized fields, and this information often adds a human touch to my topic. When the topic lends itself, I become a doer. Firsthand experience and observation give me a sense of what a topic is all about and, I believe, lend credibility to my books. I have been lucky enough to see stalactites in Carlsbad Caverns, soda straws in Kartchner Caverns, and Anasazi ruins in the cliffs at Mesa Verde National Park in Colorado.

—*Larry Dane Brimner*

Index

Numbers in *italics* indicate illustrations.

About the Author

Larry Dane Brimner has been an elementary, junior high, and high school teacher, as well as a teacher-trainer at San Diego State University. Among his more than seventy-five books for young people are several Franklin Watts titles, including these others about sports: *Mountain Biking*, *Surfing*, *Rock Climbing*, and *Snowboarding*, an IRA/CBC "Children's Choice" book. His research has put him on inline skates and taken him up rock faces, but he has never belly-crawled through a wild cave!